TOOLS FOR TEACHERS

- **ATOS:** 0.5
- **GRL:** C
- **WORD COUNT:** 30

- **CURRICULUM CONNECTIONS:** transportation

Skills to Teach

- **HIGH-FREQUENCY WORDS:** fun, have, help, on, they, us
- **CONTENT WORDS:** boats, fish, float, move, pull, sail, travel, water
- **PUNCTUATION:** exclamation point, periods
- **WORD STUDY:** long /o/, spelled oa (boats, float); /oo/, spelled o (move)
- **TEXT TYPE:** information report

Before Reading Activities

- Read the title and give a simple statement of the main idea.
- Have students "walk" though the book and talk about what they see in the pictures.
- Introduce new vocabulary by having students predict the first letter and locate the word in the text.
- Discuss any unfamiliar concepts that are in the text.

After Reading Activities

Ask children to think of other kinds of boats they know of that were not named in the text. Say their answers aloud. Encourage the children to predict the first letter of each boat name. Write their answers on the board. Tally the number of children who are familiar with each kind of boat. Ask the children what kind of purpose each boat serves.

Tadpole Books are published by Jump!, 5357 Penn Avenue South, Minneapolis, MN 55419, www.jumplibrary.com

Copyright ©2019 Jump. International copyright reserved in all countries. No part of this book may be reproduced in any form without written permission from the publisher.

Editor: Jenna Trnka **Designer:** Anna Peterson

Photo Credits: David Sacks/Getty, cover; stefann11/iStock, 1; James Pintar/iStock, 2–3, 16tm; mg7/iStock, 4–5, 16tr; LWA/Larry Williams/Getty, 6–7, 16tl; Krasowit/Shutterstock, 7 (fish); Anton Watman/Shutterstock, 8–9, 16br; cate_89/Shutterstock, 10–11, 16bl ; Prasolov Alexei/Shutterstock, 12–13, 16bm; Max Topchii/Shutterstock, 14–15.

Library of Congress Cataloging-in-Publication Data
Names: Kenan, Tessa, author.
Title: Boats / by Tessa Kenan.
Description: Minneapolis, MN : Jump!, Inc., (2018) | Series: Let's go! | Includes index.
Identifiers: LCCN 2017061695 (print) | LCCN 2018002130 (ebook) | ISBN 9781624969843 (ebook) | ISBN 9781624969829 (hardcover : alk. paper) | ISBN 9781624969836 (pbk.)
Subjects: LCSH: Boats and boating—Juvenile literature. | Ships—Juvenile literature. | CYAC: Boats and boating. | LCGFT: Picture books. | Illustrated works.
Classification: LCC VM150 (ebook) | LCC VM150 .K45 2018 (print) | DDC 623.82—dc23
LC record available at https://lccn.loc.gov/2017061695

LET'S GO!

BOATS

by Tessa Kenan

TABLE OF CONTENTS

tadpole books

BOATS

Boats float.

water

They help us move on water.

fish

They help us fish.

They help us travel.

They help us pull.

They help us sail.

They help us have fun!

WORDS TO KNOW

fish

float

move

pull

sail

travel

INDEX